Pastry On The Subway

The Adventures of Croissant on the R Train

Story and illustrations by

Carmen W. Gillespie

ISBN: 978-1-9990-3440-5

www.carmengillespie.com
https://carmengillespie.weebly.com/

*This book was inspired by a Facebook posting by
Scotty Watson (Comedian)
and comments by Val Green Field.*

Thanks, Friends!

Hi! I'm Croissant!

I get to ride the subway
all by myself to meet
with my mom today.

Will you join me?

Look! It's the R-Train!

Follow the "R"s in the
yellow circles!

It's going to be a great day!
Three guys just rapped the
weather report and it will be
sunny! Cool!

46th Street

We have a lot of time, so
we can make a few stops
on our way! Good thing my
Metrocard is loaded!

It smells funny in here, but
I like how the doors close:
"Bing-Bong!"

Let's go!

Metrocard

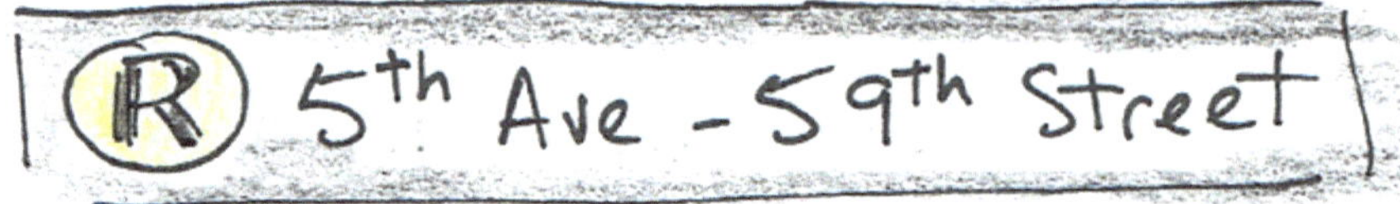

Let's hop off to look at
Central Park!

What pretty paths and bridges!
Next time I'll take a horse and
buggy ride to the carousel.

Back to the R-Train!

5
367
R
R

R
4621

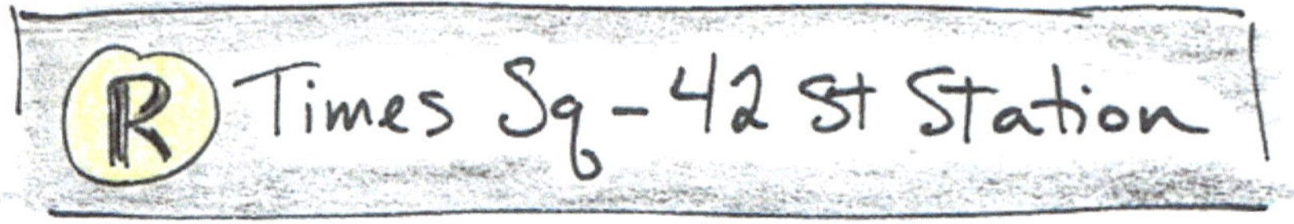

Wow! It's where the ball drops
on New Years' Eve!
Times Square has so many lights,
and the biggest TVs I have ever
seen!

Too bad we don't have time to
see a Broadway show. Next time!

Back to the R-Train!

CHOCOLATE
COME FROM AWAY
WICKED
Pharm
THEATRE
FOOD

Don't forget
your umbrella!

I ♥ NY

It's the Empire State Building,
one of the tallest in New York City!

Look! I can jump higher than the
Empire State Building...
...because buildings can't jump!
Ha ha ha!

Back to the R-Train!

EMPIRE STATE

23RD STREE

At Union Square, a lot of different train lines meet!

There's also a park, and a building with a lot of numbers on it that I don't understand, and some bakeries... The people here look hungry. Uh-oh! Stranger danger!

Let's get back to the R-Train!

140652 2607530A
?

5276

R

My mom told me to meet her at Buttery Park.

(Whoops! B_attery Park. I always say that wrong!)

And there she is! Her name is Baguette.

Hi, Mom! Ready to go to the ferry?

Wow!
Thanks for showing me the
Statue of Liberty!

She is really beautiful, and
really big!

I love that she's from France,
just like us!

That was such a great day!

Thanks for riding the R-Train
with me!

Bye-Bye!

THE
END